10 WAYS TO USE LESS PLASTIC

by Mary Boone

PEBBLE
a capstone imprint

Published by Pebble, an imprint of Capstone
1710 Roe Crest Drive, North Mankato, Minnesota 56003
capstonepub.com

Copyright © 2024 by Capstone. All rights reserved. No part of this publication may be reproduced in whole or in part, or stored in a retrieval system, or transmitted in any form or by any means, electronic, mechanical, photocopying, recording, or otherwise, without written permission of the publisher.

Library of Congress Cataloging-in-Publication Data is available on the Library of Congress website.

ISBN: 9780756577957 (hardcover)
ISBN: 9780756578084 (paperback)
ISBN: 9780756577995 (ebook PDF)

Summary: Did you know that most plastic goes to landfills instead of recycling plants? Use these 10 simple steps and added hands-on activity to reduce your plastic use and waste. Find out what tips work for you and spread the word. Together, we can make a difference!

Editorial Credits
Editor: Mandy R. Robbins; Designer: Heidi Thompson; Media Researcher: Jo Miller; Production Specialist: Tori Abraham

Image Credits
Alamy: AugustSnow, 19; Dreamstime: Kiankhoon, 14; Getty Images: Edwin Tan, 10, FluxFactory, 6, Image Source, 17, kali9, 13, LauriPatterson, 15; Shutterstock: A3pfamily, Cover (top right), fizkes, 12, Inna Reznik, Cover (top left), Jay Ondreicka, 9, kryzhov, 7, Madhourse, 18, Maslova Valentina, Cover (bottom left), MOHAMED ABDULRAHEEM, 8, Monkey Business Images, Cover (bottom right), 11, photka, 21, Vladimir Sukhachev, 16, wee design, 5

All internet sites appearing in back matter were available and accurate when this book was sent to press.

Printed and bound in China. 5593

TABLE OF CONTENTS

What Is Plastic? 4

How We Use Plastic 6

Plastic Problems 8

10 Ways You Can Use Less Plastic 10

Activity: Track Your Plastic 20

    Glossary 22

    Read More 23

    Internet Sites 23

    Index 24

    About the Author 24

Words in **BOLD** are in the glossary.

WHAT IS PLASTIC?

Plastic does not grow in nature. It is made by people. Plastic has many uses. It is strong. Plastic can be made into different shapes.

HOW WE USE PLASTIC

People use plastic in many ways. We drink from plastic cups. We store food in plastic bags. We sit on plastic chairs. We play with plastic toys. We wear plastic raincoats. Even some car parts are plastic.

PLASTIC PROBLEMS

Plastic is useful. It also causes problems. Plastic is in our **landfills**. It does not break down.

A lot of plastic ends up in rivers and oceans. Animals get confused. They think plastic garbage is food. It makes them sick. Animals get tangled in plastic nets. They get stuck in plastic rings.

10 WAYS YOU CAN USE LESS PLASTIC

1. Carry a **reusable** water bottle. Fill up at a fountain. It's an easy habit to learn.

2. Take your own bags when you shop. A single-use plastic bag takes 1,000 years to break down. Reusable bags can be used hundreds of times. Remind your family!

3. Skip the straw. Plastic straws don't break down. They are hard to **recycle**. Many straws become litter. Enjoy your drink without one. If you must use a straw, make it a reusable one.

4. Don't eat snacks that come in plastic **packaging**. Choose a piece of fruit or some veggies. Maybe you'd like a handful of nuts.

5. Say "no" to plastic packs of ketchup or mustard. If you're picking up dinner, use the sauces you have at home.

6. Pack your lunch in reusable containers. Use a thermos to carry soup or pasta. Pack salad or yogurt in a jar.

7. One billion plastic toothbrushes are thrown away each year. **Bamboo** toothbrushes break down easily. They are kinder to the environment. Will your family make the switch?

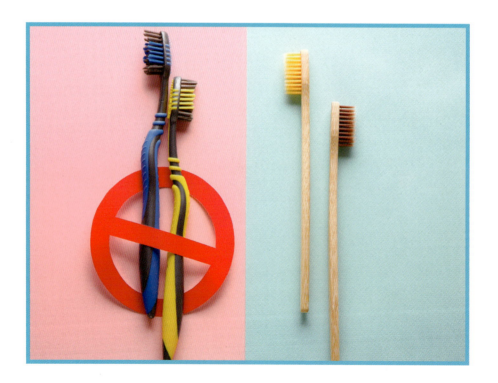

8. Do you like ice cream? Don't eat it from a cup. Choose a cone. Ice cream cups can have plastic coatings. And they usually come with plastic spoons. A cone is a cup you can eat!

9. Rub a dub dub! Use bars of soap when you shower or wash your hands. Liquid soap usually comes in plastic bottles. Bars have less plastic packaging.

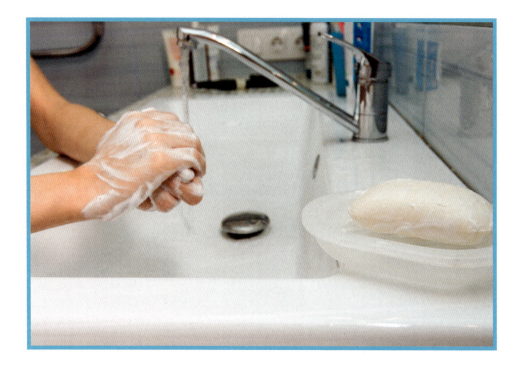

10. Need a plastic item? Check the **thrift store**. Buy a used plastic toy or container. That helps keep items out of the landfill.

No one person can save the environment. But we can all do our part. How will you cut down on plastic? How will you help the world?

19

ACTIVITY: TRACK YOUR PLASTIC

Keep track of the plastic you use during one week. What changes could you make so you're using less plastic? Try the activity again in a month and see how much less plastic you are using.

Item	Used to	Could this item be used more than one time?	Could I replace it with something not made of plastic?
Cup	Drink Milk	Yes	Yes

GLOSSARY

bamboo (bam-BOO)—a tropical grass with a hard, hollow stem; used to make items ranging from flooring and furniture to toothbrushes and utensils

landfill (LAND-fil)—a system of trash and garbage disposal in which the waste is buried between layers of earth

packaging (PACK-ij-ing)—cartons, trays, and bags used to contain items.

recycle (ree-SYE-kuhl)—to make used items into new products; people can recycle items such as rubber, glass, plastic, and aluminum

reusable (re-YOO-suh-buhl)—to use again especially in a different way

thrift store (THRIFT STOHR)—a store where people shop for donated items

READ MORE

Boone, Mary. *Recycle It!* North Mankato, MN: Capstone Press, 2021.

Boxer, Elisa. *One Turtle's Last Straw.* New York: Crown Books for Young Readers, 2022.

Hood, Susan. *The Last Straw: Kids vs. Plastics.* New York: Harper Collins, 2021.

INTERNET SITES

National Geographic Kids' Recycle Roundup
kids.nationalgeographic.com/games/action-adventure/article/recycle-roundup-new

Sustain Ability International's Ollie's World
olliesworld.com/

U.S. Environmental Protection Agency's Recycle City
epa.gov/recyclecity//

INDEX

animals, 9

bags, 6, 11

cups, 6, 17, 21

landfills, 8, 19

plastic packaging, 13, 14, 18

recycling, 12
reusable containers, 15
reusable water bottles, 10

soap, 18
straws, 12

thrift stores, 19
toothbrushes, 16

ABOUT THE AUTHOR

Mary Boone has written more than 65 nonfiction books for young readers, ranging from biographies to how-to craft guides. She grew up in rural Iowa. She now lives in Tacoma, Washington, with her husband, Mitch, and children, Eve and Eli. Mary loves being outdoors, reading, and hanging out with her Airedale terrier, Ruthie Bader.